C000060112

BE A BETTER
NURSERY NURSE

Lynn Cousins

Other titles in this series

Be a better foundation stage/nursery teacher

Be a better foundation stage coordinator

Be a better form tutor

Be a better secondary classroom teacher

Be a better teaching assistant

Be a better literacy coordinator

Be a better gifted and talented coordinator

BE A BETTER
NURSERY NURSE

by Lynn Cousins

TEACH
BOOKS

A division of MA Education Ltd

Teach Books Division, MA Education Ltd, St Jude's Church,
Dulwich Road, London SE24 0PB

British Library Cataloguing-in-Publication Data
A catalogue record is available for this book

© MA Education Limited 2006
ISBN 1 85642 322 0

Printed in the UK by Athenaeum Press Ltd, Dukesway, Team
Valley, Gateshead, NE11 0PZ

CONTENTS

INTRODUCTION

Every child in your care has potential. The potential to be a well-rounded person, with lots to offer to the community in which he lives at any particular time of his life. The potential to be creative, wise, caring, the list is endless. And you have chosen to work with children at the start of this journey. You can set children on the way to personal fulfilment.

All children in your care need protection. Protection means keeping them safe so that they can play, learn and develop in a secure place with safe adults. You can be that safe adult who offers protection, while allowing the child to take his own risks and learn the extent of his skills and abilities.

Every child in your care needs a practitioner who understands children. Someone who works with, and takes account of, the other adults in the child's life to provide a consistent and caring support system. You can be that practitioner, and this book is intended to help you to achieve this.

When you are at work do you ever stop and think? Do you make time in a busy day to pause, reflect and consider your actions or responses? If you do, then you are already a reflective practitioner.

Development and growth of ideas and understanding depend on change. If we all do things today in the same way that we did them yesterday, last week or last year, then everything will always stay the same and progress won't ever be made.

We have moved on from the days when young children worked all day in dire conditions alongside their parents. We no longer separate activities by gender. We don't expect our children to stay silent and not express their opinions or their feelings. These changes happened when those who worked with children, and for children, thought about what was happening and questioned the practice of the day – in other words they paused and reflected. They researched their facts and then shared their thoughts and the conclusions they came to. Policy changes were sometimes needed, but these all originated from someone who bothered to stop and think. Out of their work came new approaches and a better life for children.

Reflective practice is about

- developing ideas
- changing concepts
- raising standards
- gaining new levels of understanding
- expanding ideas
- extending skills.

In this book, the use of he, him or his is gender neutral and is intended to include both sexes.

CHAPTER 1

WORKING WITH PUPILS

There are two things that you should have at the forefront of your mind whenever you are working with children. The first is to be aware of their stage of development. This may seem obvious, but you should always consider what the children can do, what they are learning to do and can do at the moment with some support, and the things that are as yet too difficult for them. The second is to think about the need to build and maintain your relationships with the children. It is important that you have a relationship with each child, and that he feels at ease with you, and trusts you. Let's take each of these aspects in turn.

STAGES OF DEVELOPMENT

Whenever you work with a child you need to know where he is in terms of stage of development. Let's take an obvious example to show this: Billy is hungry. Does he need a bottle, some prepared baby food, a banana or a sandwich? The answer, of course, will depend on his stage of development.

There are many ways of describing the stages of development for any child. For example, we can look at their physical growth, their social, emotional or linguistic growth. At different times in history certain theorists have been in fashion, and their ideas have led the way and determined how we respond to children. As our knowledge has extended we have changed our thinking. As a practitioner today, you will be working with the stages of development as laid down by research which has led to the formation of some broad developmental stages. These are written down as *Birth to Three Matters* for children up to three years of age (*Box 1.1*) (DfES (Department for Education and Skills, 2002), The Foundation Stage Curriculum for children aged three to five years (*Box 1.2*) (QCA (Qualifications and Curriculum Authority, 2000), and the five outcomes as described in *Every Child Matters*, which is for all children (*Box 1.3*) (DfES, 2003).

Each time you interact with a child you should be aware of what he is currently able to do, or what he knows about this already. You must also know where you want him to get to, today, this week and in the long-term. It is the difference between these two things that you are aiming to bridge through whatever learning opportunity you are about to offer this child.

For example, at the moment Jordan can hold a chunky pencil and scribble random marks on paper. You want him to be able to write his name - eventually. To get from where he is now to achieving this long-term aim, he first needs to master:

- *controlling the direction of his pencil*
- *pressing the pencil down firmly.*

Of course, he also needs to learn the letters and how to form them, but you are concentrating on the fine motor skills today, so you will provide opportunities for him to practise his pencil control. Colouring in shapes and outlines will help him to coordinate his hand with his eye. Completing jigsaws, painting, playing with dough or fitting Duplo together will also help him develop these skills.

Box 1.1. Birth to Three Matters

Birth to Three Matters describes the child's development during these years in four stages:

Heads Up, Lookers and Communicators:
Young babies from 0–8 months:
- respond to other people with their whole body
- can observe and respond to their immediate environment
- can communicate with people around them.

Sitters, Standers and Explorers:
Babies from 8–18 months:
- explore their environment intentionally
- become increasingly mobile
- start to develop language
- find out about and understand more of their world.

Movers, Shakers and Players:
Young children from 18–24 months:
- show increasing independence
- take pleasure in moving and communicating
- enjoy learning through play.
  Walkers, Talkers and Pretenders:

Children from 24–36 months:
- are competent at moving, talking and pretending
- show increasing confidence in themselves
- become skilled in making relationships

Each of these is defined in general terms, and you will have to find the best fit for any child in your care.

Box 1.2. The foundation stage profile

The foundation stage curriculum is divided into six areas of learning. Each of these areas has a number of steps (stepping stones) towards a defined goal (early learning goals). Children will not achieve these steps in an even manner. They will know a bit of one and part of another. They may know some that seem to come later before some earlier steps. They will know something today and forget it another day. But you need to be aware of the route along which they are developing, even if they cover it in a zigzag fashion and not in the straight line that would make your life so much easier.

Box 1.3. The five outcomes for children

From the green paper *Every Child Matters* many changes have been made to the ways in which we work with and respond to children. There is now a shared vision of what children can expect; these are known as the five outcomes for children. They must be included in all of our planning and will be inspected by Ofsted. The five outcomes are that each child will:

- be healthy
- stay safe
- enjoy and achieve
- make a positive contribution
- achieve economic wellbeing.

DEVELOPING RELATIONSHIPS WITH THE CHILDREN

Establishing trust depends on having a positive relationship with another person. There are three areas where you can work on building up a trusting relationship with the children in your care. These are:

1. Containment
2. Consistency
3. Communication

Containment

Containment is the holding in of the energy of an emotion.

For example, you get up one morning to an argument with your partner. This upsets your son who cries and clings as you try to

5

leave for work. You arrive at work tense, anxious and upset. George comes in and starts touching the paper you have just laid out for a writing session you are going to do with the children this morning. He scribbles on one sheet. What do you do?

It is at this point that you need to exercise containment. You need to hold in your first response which might have been to be cross with George, to snatch up the paper, to shout at him. But George didn't know it was special paper, he saw crayons and pencils and paper and he did what you often expect of him – he drew a picture.

Containment stops you transferring your emotions to the children. Young children are very much mind–body linked. They can easily be disturbed by emotional responses. If you show your anxiety, the children in turn will become anxious. If you are cross, they can pick up on this and respond with their own cross behaviour, or they can be afraid of you and respond by withdrawing. Lack of containment on your part can lead to losing a child's trust.

Helping children to learn containment

Children need help if they are to learn to contain their own emotions, whether anxiety, anger or excitement. To do this you need to remain calm. You should keep your voice quiet, speak slowly and unemotionally. Don't rise to the bait of the child's emotion. The child will be displaying all his emotions, but whatever he says, whatever he does, you must not over-react to it. If he is to regain control of his emotions, and to contain the energy of those emotions, he needs to have a quiet, firm, reassuring adult supporting him. On some occasions you will be successful simply by speaking and acting calmly. But there will be occasions when you have to transfer from verbal containment of the emotions to physical containment.

Physical containment

There may be times when you have to bring other consequences into play.

> *For example, Ewan hits several other children because he doesn't want to share the sand tray. He has to go and sit in the time-out place – an identified chair, square of carpet or cushion. He must stay there for one or two minutes, whatever is the agreed policy in your setting. Have a timer and be precise about this length of time. Place the timer where Ewan can see it so that he can see time passing; remember that children of this age don't have a well-established sense of time and won't know what two minutes feel like. During that time no-one will give him any eye contact or speak with him. If he moves away, he will be taken back – still with no eye contact or exchange of words – until the agreed time is up. Do this as often as necessary. When the time is up, still speaking calmly, you will tell him that he can now return to his previous activity.*

It is not productive to explain things to the child or try to discuss his behaviour while he is in a state of heightened emotions. He won't be able to absorb your message. Wait until he is calm, the incident well past, and then introduce it into the conversation. Explain calmly: 'when you do this ... I will do this ... because when you do ... it hurts children (or damages something or upsets someone...)'.

Use circle time to talk with the children as a group about how we behave, good or bad responses and the consequences of unacceptable behaviour. Don't refer back to any specific child or incident when you do this. Talk in general terms or use a puppet to act out the inappropriate behaviour, and then show a better way to have behaved. Let the children handle the puppet and let them practise the behaviour you want to see.

On rare occasions a child's emotions may be so out of control that you will need to physically hold him until you sense that he has calmed down (*Box 1.4*). If you let him go and he repeats the behaviour take hold of him again. Repeat this as often as it takes to calm the child. When he is calm, act normally with him. Wash his face if he has been crying, reassure him that everything has returned to normal and then let him go off to play.

Box 1.4. Containing a child physically

You will have guidelines that you must follow in your setting. These will have been worked out in line with child protection awareness. It is important that you know these strategies and use only the ones written down in your behaviour policy. Ways of doing this could include:

- Sit the child on a small chair, stand behind it and place your hand gently on his shoulder.
- Sit the child on a small chair at a table and stand behind so that he can't push it back and get up.
- Sit the child on a seat next to you and hold his hand.

Always stay behind or beside the child, never in front, as you want to avoid eye contact. Don't chat with the child during this time or try to reprimand him. If he moves away, calmly but firmly bring him back.

Remember: we all have our own concept of personal space. We all have a comfort zone. We don't all like being held. Some don't like to be too close to another person. Respect the child's individual sense of personal space. Don't confuse this with a child simply trying to avoid the consequences of his behaviour.

Anna may not like being touched. So if you put a hand on her shoulder she may squirm. Remove the hand and she may well stay in the time out seat anyway.

Consistency

Whatever your mood, whatever problems you are facing at home, you must leave all this behind you when you come into the nursery or other setting where you work.

Compare these two responses:

Alex is playing with paint. He is supposed to be painting a house for the display everyone is creating. He paints the palms of his hands and places them on his paper. Emily is working with this group. She sees what he has done and comments that although these are very interesting and 'look we can see all of his fingers' she then reminds him about the task in hand, provides a clean piece

of paper and puts the hand prints to dry. Alex then paints a house very carefully.

That night Emily falls out with her best friend, is upset, and doesn't sleep well. She sleeps in and is late getting up. She arrives at nursery in a rush, having forgotten her lunch. Alex is painting. He is supposed to be painting a car to go on the street scene. He decides to paint his hands again as his mummy liked the prints he took home yesterday. Emily sees him. 'That's naughty,' she tells him. 'Stop it.' She takes his paper, throws it away and tells him to go and get another piece. Alex is upset, he leaves the table and refuses to paint any more today.

When we interact with a child in our care we first of all have to build a relationship with that child. The actions we take and the words we use will determine what sort of relationship it is going to be. This is going to build over time. When the child knows that we will be fair and responsive, then he starts to offer us his trust. When children trust us, then we can support their development in every way. Alex is not sure of Emily. He can't trust her reactions, and this will affect their relationship.

Reliability helps to build up trust

The child needs to know that he can trust you. If he sees you every day, if he gets a smile and a positive response from you each day, then he will see you as someone to trust. The child needs to know that when he comes to nursery you will be there. If you know you are going to be away, on holiday or on a course, for example, let him know about it. Tell him where you are going and why, and when he can expect to see you again. Let him know who will be there for him when you are away.

There is also an element of honesty in this. If children know the truth they can usually cope. It is the unknown which most worries children.

Communication

Think about the words that you say and the way that you say them.

Never use sarcasm with young children at this age. They can't distinguish between your response to their actions and your response to them as a person. At this young age, if you criticise their drawing you criticise the child.

Body language

Your body language can be a reflection of your true feelings and the child can just as easily pick up on this.

Try this: when you see a baby who you don't know, smile at him with your mouth only, and watch his response. Now try it again, but this time make your eyes twinkle, or give a little wink as well as smiling with your mouth. The response from the baby should be very different.

When you are working with children come down to their level, sit at the sand tray, don't stand towering over the children. Sit on the floor with a group who are playing there. Kneel down to talk with a child who is trying hard to share some important news with you. When you read a story, sit on a low chair or a bean-bag.

Listening to children

Children need time to express themselves. Make sure that you allow for this. If you ask a question, leave plenty of time for their

answer. Prompt them as they explain with lots of encouraging words. 'Did you? And then what happened?' and similar phrases encourage them to develop their thoughts and ideas. It also helps them to order their thinking and tell a story or relate an incident in a structured manner.

Be alert to the meaning behind the words. Are they trying to tell you something? They may not have all of the words to express their emotional needs, so they may tell you about something that has happened. You will need to ask the right questions to get to the point.

> *'I took my cat Sooty to the vet last night. The vet kept him there'.*

> *This could be his way of telling you that he is worried, or upset. Perhaps mummy was crying. Sooty may even have died or may do so in the next day or two.*

Find out so that you can help the child to cope. The child has recognised you as someone he could trust with this information. Build on this and show that his trust was placed in the right person, who will deal sensitively with his needs.

Conversation

Communication is a two-way process. It involves listening as well as speaking. When you are talking with one child or a small group, think about the balance of the conversation.

- Are you talking more often than the children?
- Are you asking questions to which the children will know, or not know the correct answer?
- Do you ask questions that are open ended: 'What do you think this might be?' rather than closed, 'What colour is this?'
- Do you answer questions with more questions to develop the child's thinking?
- Do you initiate all of the conversations?
- Do you encourage your children to ask lots of questions?
- Do you take those questions seriously and try to find out the answers together?
- Do you help the shy ones to contribute?
- Do you praise their attempts at speech?

Ask a colleague to observe you. Ask her to note how often you engage a child in conversation compared with how often you simply instruct or give orders: 'Come down from there', 'Put those away' or 'Put your coat on'.

Handy Hints

- You need to understand the different stages of development.
- Develop relationships with the children.
- Know the children in terms of their development.
- Know what you want the children to learn.
- Plan to bridge this gap.
- Build up good relationships with children through containment, consistency and communication.

CHAPTER 2

KEEPING ON TOP OF YOUR SUBJECT AREA

Lesley Abbott and Anne Langston (2005), writing in *Birth to Three Matters*, sum up the argument of others in these words.

> *'The key to quality experiences and provision for young children depends on the quality of the adults who work with them....'*

However experienced you are, and whatever the level of your training, it is important that you continue to learn and to think about children and how they develop and learn, and about how you work with them and support them to foster their development, throughout your career. A phrase that sums this up well is that you should be a 'reflective practitioner'.

THE REFLECTIVE PRACTITIONER

This is someone who thinks about what they do, why they do it and how they could do it better. There are two main areas on which to focus these reflections:

- How the children in your care learn and develop, and how you can encourage and enable this to happen in ever more effective ways.
- How you can continue to become an ever more effective practitioner.

Stop and think

To be reflective you have to start by allowing yourself time to stop and think. This needs to happen at all stages of the learning cycle: when you are planning activities, when you are setting out the room and working with the children, when you are observing and assessing them, and, probably most importantly, when you are evaluating the experiences and learning which have taken place (*Box 2.1*).

Talk with others

You need to talk with others. They could be colleagues in your setting, members of a support group you belong to or fellow participants on a course you are attending. These could be formal or informal discussions.

Scheduled staff meetings can be a time to talk with your colleagues and share your thoughts. You may have a subject that is giving you cause for concern, or that you want to know more about, or you may want to suggest a new approach you would like to consider using. Plan these subjects in advance so that everyone knows what they are going to talk about. Post a notice on the staff room board: 'Next Tuesday, 4th October, we will be discussing ideas for using the sand tray for a wider range of activities'. One member of the team could prepare some information and lead the discussion. You could arrange for an expert to come in and talk to the whole team.

Box 2.1. Questions to ask yourself

When planning
- Is the planning document itself a usable format?
- What level of detail is actually useful?

When setting out the room
- Is this the best place for this activity? Would the room flow better if we moved things to other places?
- Is this display clearly visible to the children?

When working with the children
- If I sat at the other side of the table would I be able to keep an eye on another group?
- Can the children hear me? Should we be next to a quieter activity?

When assessing the children
- Do I have a tight enough focus for this assessment?
- Is this way of recording the assessment too wordy?
- I'm not sure why Sam is behaving like this, I must ask someone or read up about children with this condition.

Evaluating the week
- Did that activity actually allow the children to practise that skill?
- Would it have been better if we had changed those two activities around and done that one first?

Time to read

Do make time to read. Professional publications are full of information about new thinking and different approaches, as well as containing practical suggestions. They can be expensive, so plan your purchases. Each member of the team could buy a different publication and then pass it around. Initial the ones you have read and make a note on any article you find particularly useful or would like to keep. Set up a concertina folder and place articles in under various headings: for example child development, reading or baby care. Once a year sort it out and throw away anything that hasn't been used. Keep reflecting.

Books are plentiful. Go through the contents page in a critical way, read a few pages from sections of the book and then decide if you want to buy it. Having bought it, set time aside to read it, time when you are fresh enough to think about the content. Use post-its to mark interesting paragraphs that you may want to come back to, or keep a notebook in which you can note down any ideas or snatches of information which you would consider using – with a page reference so that you can look it up again. Or use a soft pencil and mark the book itself.

There are websites which you can visit to find out more about children and their developmental needs, and to find professional support. At the end of this book there are some suggestions for websites which are particularly relevant.

What changes could you make to your practice to become a truly reflective practitioner?

Take this pattern, which will be familiar to most people who work in nurseries and classrooms.

■ The practitioner works, sometimes on her own, with her own group of children.

■ From time to time, she reflects on what she does each day.

■ She attends courses occasionally, finds them exciting, but when she returns to work...

■ She continues to work as she has always done.

This can be the result of feeling over-burdened or overwhelmed by all the daily routines. It could also be the sign of a practitioner who doesn't care any more. Let's look at this again, and point out ways in which this routine can be improved.

■ The practitioner works, sometimes on her own, with her own group of children.

■ She regularly reflects on what she does each day.

■ She attends courses occasionally, finds them exciting, and notes down ideas that she can use tomorrow, next week or in the future on her course notes. She may do this during the course or when she gets home.

■ On returning to work she talks with her colleagues about her thoughts for including some of the ideas. Or she shares the information with her colleagues at the next staff

meeting. She can, for instance, suggest new routines which could be adopted in their setting to encourage the creation of a learning community.

- She monitors the impact of any changes to make sure that they are benefiting the children's learning, staff attitudes or whatever the focus of the change was.
- Standards of care and learning are improved for the children. The practitioner has shown that she is a reflective practitioner and an asset to the setting.

Appraisal: a way to reflect on your practice, your skills and your knowledge

This can happen in two ways

1. You could be appraised by your line manager: this will be part of a formal process.

2. You can appraise yourself, either as part of the formal process, before you meet with your line manager, or as part of your personal reflective practice.

There will be a system already in place in your setting for appraisal, performance management or professional development interviews. The title may be different but the essence of the activity remains the same. (To make it easier to read, the term 'appraisal' is used throughout this section.) You and your line manager want to know:

■ What skills and knowledge do you have?
■ What skills and knowledge do you need to have to do this job or to prepare for more responsibility?
■ How will you acquire those skills and that knowledge?

The skills and knowledge you are expected to have will be set out in the professional standards for those working with children.

Appraisal is also worth carrying out on a less formal basis, but still at regular intervals, so that you can keep track of your own professional development.

Benefits to be gained from appraisal

- taking stock of your job and your current role
- thinking about your career prospects
- allowing time for reflection and analysis
- raising awareness of your skills, your attitudes, your knowledge, your potential
- matching your role to your job description
- highlighting areas for development
- identifying your strengths

- enabling you to plan future actions or set targets
- keeping your CV up-to-date in case you want to look for another post.

Carrying out your self-appraisal

Let's imagine that you carried out a self-appraisal at this time last year, and that in discussion with your line manager you planned some actions that you could take to increase your skills and knowledge; perhaps some courses you needed to attend, or some help that the more experienced staff could offer you. Look back at your appraisal record and then try to respond to the questions below, or reflect upon them. Be honest with yourself as you do this, as that is the only way to gain from the process.

Honesty and confidentiality

If you are then going to go on to discuss this with your line manager, there should be an understanding that if you acknowledge or draw attention to any deficiencies in your skill base, for example, that you want to address, then this information should be seen in this light only. You need to know that it will not be used in any way against you, now or in the future. For example, it should not be used as a basis for complaints about your competency. This, and the whole issue of confidentiality between you and your appraiser, should be an over-arching principle of the appraisal process.

Use these questions as you carry out your self-appraisal

1. What have I accomplished since my last appraisal?
   Look back at your targets, or the actions you planned to take and respond to these next questions for each target in turn:

- Have you met the target?

- Have you partially met the target, and if so, identify how far you have come, and whether you aim to continue working towards this particular target?

- Is there any target that you have been unable to meet? If so, identify why this happened. Did you set too many targets? Did your role change so that you were unable to take on this target at this time?

- Did you change your mind? Do you want to aim for this target again, either as it was set last year or with some changes? Is it now irrelevant?

2. Could I improve my performance?

- List the roles you carry out regularly. Now look at your job description. Do these match? Are you doing the job you are supposed to be doing? Are you doing it more, less or differently?

- Have you got any particular professional skills or relevant knowledge that you are not using? Why aren't you using them? Does you line manager know about them? Are there any opportunities in this setting for using them?

- Is there anything in your job description that you can't do? What additional skills or knowledge would you need to have? Could you identify these as your targets for the coming year?

- Is there any new responsibility you would like to take on in the future, either in the short-term or the long-term?

- Do you need any additional skills or knowledge to do this? Find out where and how you could get them; think about training, courses, support from colleagues.

- Is there anything that your line manager or another staff member could do to help you to improve your performance?

You could make notes about your self-appraisal

One easy-to-read format is to do a strengths, weaknesses, opportunities and threats (SWOT) analysis, simply making notes under each of these headings as you evaluate your current professional position.

Strengths	Weaknesses
Opportunities	Threats

Meeting with your line manager

The information here is written for you when you are being appraised by your line manager. There may be a time when you are the line manager and you are appraising one of your colleagues, and this information would be equally valid to you then.

Talk about

- your past performance
- your job description
- any observations that your line manager carried out on you
- your targets and how far they have been achieved.

Discuss

- things or people that have helped you professionally over the past year
- anything (or anyone) which has hindered you over the past year
- how these could be turned into positive experiences this next year

- any training that you have undertaken and how it did or did not benefit you professionally.

Plan

- your targets
- training needs
- actions you need to take over the next year.

Rewrite

- any aspects of your job description that need changing.

Review

Arrange some dates to meet your line manager over the next year:

- to identify the steps you have made towards your targets
- your next appraisal meeting.

After your appraisal

You should have a formal system in your setting (*Box 2.2*). Your line manager will give you a copy of the notes about what you discussed and the targets you have agreed. Keep this in a safe place. It should be in a file you use often, so that it remains in your sight and so that you remember to make it happen.

Appraisal which has simply looked back over the past year serves little purpose. You need to think about your targets and your future, and together with your line manager look for any courses, and apply for them. Find out about any other settings you could visit to see how others do things. Look for books or on-line ideas to increase your knowledge.

Box 2.2.

Trust and confidentiality should be a major principle in the appraisal process. Information given here should not be divulged to a third party without the full agreement of both parties.

Did you agree the focus of any observations to be made of your practice? These should be linked to your targets.

Appraisal can be a formal process or a tool for self-improvement

Appraisal is about learning and improving

Setting targets for your professional development

Targets should be specific, measurable and achievable. When you carry out your next self-appraisal, these simple guidelines will help make it much easier to measure whether or not you have achieved your targets. For each of these, look at the two targets against the given criteria. Notice how the second one in each case will allow you to check your progress more easily at your next appraisal. When you set your targets bear these in mind.

Be very specific

- to become better at planning

OR

- to find out about different ways of recording planning and talk to the staff about them, so that we can find a way that works well for us all.

Make it measurable

- to learn more about first aid

OR

- to achieve my first aid at work certificate.

Make it achievable

You may want to lead a team, or take charge of one area of the nursery eventually, but there are smaller steps you need to master first in the shorter term to lead to your long-term goal.

- to lead a team

OR

- to become a mentor to a trainee.

Who is responsible for your professional development?

Fundamentally, you are. You have to have the motivation to want to improve. You must be ready to take up any opportunities that are offered by your manager. You must be willing to see yourself as a lifelong learner (*Box 2.3*).

It is essential that you become pro-active. One of the things that sets us apart from other animals is our ability to evaluate ourselves, to think about what we do, how we behave and how we feel. We can decide to behave, act or think in certain ways. In this case, we can decide to progress in our chosen career, and, having made this decision, we can take steps to make it happen.

To sum up

A reflective practitioner will

- stop and think
- talk with others
- make time to read
- use appraisal as a means of developing her own practice.

Box 2.3.

'There is no resting on your laurels even when you have achieved a high degree of skill...' (Blakemore and Frith, 2005).

They describe a study which was carried out on a group of people who were taught to juggle. They practised with three balls for at least one minute per day for three months. Their brains were scanned and the areas concerned with visual motion information were shown to have changed over this period of time. Over the next three months they didn't practise and their brain scans showed that they lost all of the previously seen changes. In other words – use it or lose it.

Handy Hints

- Learn how to become a reflective practitioner.
- Appraisal should be used as a means of reflecting on your practice, skills and knowledge.
- You can undertake self-appraisal using SWOT analysis.
- Make sure that you set targets and follow-up to make sure they're being met.

CHAPTER 3

ACTIVITIES

In this chapter we will look at the four stages of activities:

1. Planning and preparation
2. Delivery
3. Assessment
4. Evaluation.

These four aspects form a cycle, with each one informing the next stage and developing from the previous one.

PLANNING AND PREPARATION

In every aspect of our lives we can see the benefits of planning. You have decided to move house: where would you like to move to? How much can you afford? Can you get the right mortgage? Are there decent schools nearby for your own children? Can you get to work in reasonable time? And then there are the surveys, the removal firm, and so on. Without planning this would be an even greater headache.

Focus on the children

When you construct the plans for the children in your care you are bringing to these plans all the information you already hold about these children. You use the results of your assessments to recognise where the children are, in terms of skills and knowledge, and think about where you want them to be and how you can help them to get there. You will be including the evaluations you have made on how well this activity went down last time you used it, or about whether a particular activity allowed the child to learn what you had hoped he would from it. Just by focusing on the children, their achievements and their future needs you will be learning so much more about them. Planning with your colleagues instead of on your own gives you an opportunity to share this information and helps to broaden each person's understanding of that child or that group of children.

Modifying your plans

Each year you will have to write the plans anew because they must always reflect the children. Of course they have to cover the content of the curriculum, but this should always be shaped and moulded to the needs of these particular children. If you keep

the plans you already have, these will make a good starting point. It is much easier to start with something down on paper – a blank sheet of paper is a very hard place to start. Take your original plans, and adapt them as necessary. If the order in which you presented the activities didn't work well, change it. If you found that a certain activity was too hard for most of the children, think about keeping it back until later in the year when they will have matured a little more (*Boxes 3.1* and *3.2*).

Routines

Routines are good for children. They help them to make sense of a world which is full of excitement, novelty and new experiences. Children feel safe with a routine, knowing what is going to happen and anticipating their favourite parts of the day.

Routines are good for you, because they help you to keep track of all the things that have to be done. You don't have to stop and think 'What do I do next?' if one activity regularly follows on another. When children have a routine, even the most reticent child can be adventurous within it. Children know the boundaries and can play within them until they feel secure enough to push those boundaries and stretch their level of competence, testing out their new skills. The daily routines will help to structure your plans. This doesn't mean that every day has to be exactly the same as the one before it. For example, every day you will have a time for sitting as a group. You could change the place where you sit:

> '*This week we are doing lots of things about growing things, so we are going to sit in the garden near the flowers we have planted to read the story of "The Seed".*'

> '*This week we have been thinking about dark and light, so we are going to sit in this dark corner today, with the light out, and we will have some torches and sing some songs together.*'

Box 3.1. Plans you will need

- Long-term plans: these give an overview of the whole year. Make sure that you cover all areas of learning.
- Medium-term plans: these give a more detailed picture of the activities you will include in any week, month or half-term, and the resources you will need. Make sure that you cover all of the early learning goals.
- Short-term plans: these give details about specific activities for identified groups of children. Make sure that you cover all the stepping stones.

Box 3.2. Keeping your plans

- Put the long-term plan somewhere where all of the staff can see it, on a notice board in your staffroom for example
- Keep a folder or binder of medium-term plans for each section of your nursery, one folder per room
- Have a copy of the short-term plan which covers this week or sometimes just one day, for each member of the team. Have a copy where parents can see it.

None of these plans should be viewed as a completed, never-to-be-touched-again sort of document. They are working documents and as such you should be able to write on them 'this worked', 'this didn't work', 'changed this and it worked better' or 'did this instead of that'.

To sum up

Plans will help you

- You will know what equipment you need to have available.
- You can prepare any additional materials or find out where you can borrow or buy things you might need.
- If you suddenly get a good idea for an activity, you can find the appropriate plan and make a note of your idea, ready for next time you use that plan.

Plans will help the children

- They will sense the orderly atmosphere and will feel safe and secure.
- They will know what to expect from the normal routine.
- Changes to the routine will be pleasant surprises.
- They can anticipate their favourite activities or plan for tomorrow.

Plans will help the team

- Everyone will know what they are doing and what they will be responsible for over the week.
- You will be able to accommodate people's strengths. 'Carly's mum said she can come in on the first Tuesday of each month and she's really good at cooking, so we could plan to make the pizzas with the children that day.'
- If someone is unexpectedly absent you can re-arrange the allocation of responsibilities, and not have to panic at the last moment because 'Shelley was going to find something for the science table and she hasn't turned up, and we don't know what she was going to do.'

DELIVERY

Learning at this stage doesn't take place in small compartments. We can't teach science as a separate entity from language, social skills or fine motor development. Whatever the child is doing, he is learning something – whether we want him to learn that particular thing or not.

Every moment of the day is an opportunity for learning. Some of the learning will be incidental, some will be planned, some will be child-led and some will be adult-led. Your role will vary. You could be

- a facilitator
- an observer
- an instructor.

Consider your role

Facilitator

When children are playing you can intervene to make sure that all the children are having equal access to the equipment or that everyone is taking turns. You can point out to the children a new way of doing something: 'Have you tried putting the paint on with this fatter brush?'. The children are leading the play, but you are enabling that play to happen in constructive ways for maximum learning and enjoyment.

Sometimes a child brings in something to share with the others. They all show such interest that you decide to let the children pursue the subject. As a facilitator you can provide materials and opportunity to enlarge upon this: a bridesmaid's headpiece might develop into a hat shop, or a visit to the seaside might result in everyone planning a journey – possibly even going on a journey.

Observer

Sometimes you will be formally observing the children as part of the assessment programme. Sometimes you will want to step back and observe, just to make sure that all is going well. The children are busy with an activity, they are making good use of the equipment and working well together. You will simply be keeping a monitoring view of them for safety's sake.

Instructor

This is when you will be much more focused on a group of children, what they are doing and what they are learning. Your role is to explain the activity, to describe to them what they should be able to do or what they will know by the end of this activity, and then to support them as they carry out the activity. At the end of the activity you can remind them about what they have learnt, what they can now do and praise them for all their hard work and concentration.

Know your material

It is important that you are familiar with the curriculum, either *Birth to Three Matters* (QCA, 2000) or the Foundation Stage curriculum (DfES, 2002). When you complete your plans for the day, check which aspects of these you expect the children to practise, learn or acquire. Make a note of these on your plan so that you keep them in mind. It is easy to be diverted when working with children. It is good to follow these alternative routes at times, but you should remain aware of your original intention and bring the children's attention back to that if possible. If you don't, then make sure that you note this down on the plan so that you can tackle that aspect again another day.

Where does this activity fit in?

As well as knowing each child's stage of development you need to remain aware of the development of this aspect of learning.

- What will the children have already experienced? Remind them of this before you start.

- Where can they go next? If you start the activity and then discover one or more of the children can already do this, or learn to do it quite quickly, you may need to embark on the next step. If you don't, children can soon become bored, and bored children can quickly disrupt the activity by messing about.

- How does this link with other areas of learning? Remind the children of something they did earlier.

Making connections

Children learn more effectively when they can see the connections between aspects of their learning. Help them to do this by drawing their attention to it.

Links to prior learning allow you to tune the children into an activity. It reminds them of what they already know. It helps you to find out who has remembered and it gives you a chance to go over that information with the children to refresh their minds.

Useful phrases for the start of an adult-led activity (*Box 3.3*):

'Do you remember when.....?'

'Who saw the...?'

'On Tuesday we went to.... and we saw....Well, today we are going to.....'

Links with other skills or knowledge can help the children to make sense of what they are learning.

> *'When we were making the big model car outside on Monday, do you remember that we had a bit of a problem? Who can remember what that problem was?' Draw out the children's thoughts to establish that you couldn't get the wheels to go round. 'Well, I've collected up lots of toy cars and we are going to look at them very carefully and see whether the wheels work and how they do this.'*

> *You can now introduce words such as 'axle' and look at how these are fixed on. After this session the children may wish to look again at the big model and adapt the original wheels.*

**Box 3.3. Delivering an adult-led activity,
acting as instructor**

Explain the intention of the activity so that children can start to
focus their own thinking:

- Today we are going to use these objects to find out what they
feel like. You may learn some new words as we do this.

Describe the activity so that the children know what to do:

- Take one piece each and then I'm going to ask each
of you in turn if you can tell me what your piece feels
like. Vocabulary development will follow as the children
contribute new descriptive words: soft, sharp, rough,
smooth, bumpy, cold.

Develop the activity, describing to the children how this
will work:

- Now we are going to put all the things back into this bag,
and I am going to choose one and describe it to you. Keep
to the words you have been learning, such as soft and
smooth. Can the children guess which object you have
chosen?

Assess the children's learning by letting each one in turn have
a go.

- Can they describe things by their texture? Can they use
vocabulary in interesting and appropriate ways?

Inclusion

As you set up activities you will have to make sure that all the
children can be included. Do you have any children who
experience difficulties with access?

- Can they all reach up to a table or down to the car track marked out in the play ground?
- Can everyone see this far away?
- Have you got scissors that everyone can use, or some adapted ones for those who may need them?
- You may have to use a signer with hearing-impaired children. Have you set the activity up so that the extra adult can get in, be in the right place and in view?
- Check for allergies before handling food, pets or plants.

To sum up

- Decide on your role in the children's learning.
- Know your material and your equipment.
- Help the children to see where this learning fits into the bigger picture.
- Make sure that all of the children can access the activities.

ASSESSMENT

Assessment enables you first to discover what the children already know, so that you can decide on the next activity, and then it can be used as a way of finding out what the children have learned from that activity.

Assessing what the children have learned

You will be assessing the children all the time in an informal way. For example, you are watching the children cut out some shapes for a collage they are making about a garden. You notice that Ali can't manage the scissors very well. His paper is tearing and he is getting frustrated, so you find him a pair of scissors with a different grip. He can use these well and successfully cuts out some shapes. This was an informal assessment.

■ You set out an activity.
■ You observed the children at the activity.
■ You observed a child unable to do this activity.
■ You adapted the activity to suit the child's level of fine motor development.

You will also assess the children in a more formal way. You should have a plan which means that every child is assessed on a regular basis. There are different ways of approaching this. You could:

1. Have a card index with each child's name, date of birth and key worker written on individual cards. On the back of the card list the six areas of learning as identified in the Foundation Stage curriculum (Creative development = CD; Communication language and literacy = CLL; Knowledge and understanding of the world = KUW; Mathematical development = MD; Physical development = PD; Personal social and emotional development = PSED). Arrange the cards in their box so that the key workers' names are in a sequence, Emily, Kate, Nimisha, Julie, Emily, Kate, Nimisha, Julie, etc. Each day, each key worker could take the next card with her name on, and assess that child, replacing the card at the back of the box at the end of the assessment. The area for assessment may be determined by the activities for the day, but by putting a date against the area of learning you will be able to check that you have assessed all areas on a regular basis.

This is a good way to keep a check on the assessments being carried out, to make sure that all areas are covered, and that the child is being regularly assessed.

FRONT

> Gracie Barlow
> 24.05.03
> Key worker: Emily

BACK

> Foundation Stage
> PSED   17/03/05, 21/05/05
> CLL   05/02/05, 18/03/05, 26/04/05
> MD   10/03/05, 15/04/05
> KUW   06/03/05, 29/03/05, 11/04/05
> PD   14/03/05, 27/05/05
> CD   30/03/05, 16/05/05

2. Target one area of the foundation stage each week. This would ensure that each area is covered every six weeks. On your weekly plan highlight the area to be assessed each week. Over the week each key worker could assess her own children. Alternatively, one adult could be designated to carry out all the assessments over the week and then report back to key workers at the end of the week. The key workers could take this information and record it on their own children's records. Benefits from this approach include: the worker who is assessing gets a whole picture; she can concentrate on assessment and record-keeping for part of each day; she can focus on the learning intentions of the activity and make sure that the assessment is carried out fairly.

3. Identify the learning intentions for each activity. Post this up next to the activity. If it is written on a large piece of paper (*Box 3.4*), taking up only a small amount of the

available space, any adult working with any child in that area can jot down an assessment of the child's response to the activity. At the end of the day, key workers can collate the information referring to their own children.

**Box 3.4 Example of learning intentions
for an activity**

Today in the house we are
Setting the table for the dolls to have a party
We will be learning
Matching the number of plates, cups etc to the number of dolls seated at the table. *[Mathematical development: Calculating: compare two groups of objects, saying when they have the same number]*

Kelly could do this
Jamie needed help if there were more than 3 dolls
Jack needed help

Assessing how the children learn

You can also assess the children's approach to learning. By observing them you will be able to see how they learn. You will notice those who have a go and then give up. Some will be seen to persevere, sticking at something, determined to be successful. Some children will try lots of different ways in a haphazard fashion, while others work methodically through all the options.

This information will help you to be aware of how the children are learning. It may guide you in the way you can become involved in children's learning. If you watch their approach to a task you may be able to intervene to show them an alternative way.

'If you hold the paper this way while you are cutting it out, you will be able to see the lines you are trying to follow.'

'If you check each one in turn you will know which things you have already tried to float.'

Assess children in different situations

During the day any child may be working alone, with a friend, in a group of his own choosing, or a group you have put together. Observe him in all of these settings. One of the foundation stage stepping stones for PSED is that a child should be able to 'relate and make attachments to members of their group'. You had noted that Amy wasn't doing this when you had a group of children round the fish tank talking to them about the way the fish hide. But then you notice her with her own friends in the house and she is making excellent contact and relating very well. Remember that children are whole people, and they need to be seen in all their groupings, and in different circumstances before you can make a true judgment about them.

Keeping assessment records

The most important thing about keeping assessment records is that they should be usable (*Box 3.5*). You don't want anything that takes too much reading. If you are handed one sheet of paper you will probably read it. If you are handed a file of papers you are more likely to say, 'I'll look at that that when I have time' and we all know that in our busy schedules that time may never be found.

Box 3.5 Keeping assessment records

- Make them short and to the point.
- Record what the children can do.
- Keep evidence of their achievements.
- Note down any specific problems children may have.

Record what the children can do. You need to know when they have achieved a stepping stone or an early learning goal. Make a note of the date, and record any additional information, such as what they said or did, that showed you their achievement.

> *12/05/05 PSED: Behaviour and self control: show care and concern for others*
>
> *Cara shared her crayons with Anna when there weren't enough pots of crayons to go round.*

You don't always need to know what they can't do. So if you assessed a group of children and found that three of them could do this, note it down. 'On this day, this child could do this thing.' If the other two in the group couldn't do it, simply indicate that you assessed them and date the records.

If a child continues to be unable to do something after several assessments you will want to look into this further, as he may need some additional help. The dates will be useful as they will show for how long this child has been trying to learn this new skill or acquire this knowledge. If a child can't achieve something because of a specific problem that you notice, then it is worth recording this. It will help you to adapt the equipment or your approach. It might help you to plan a different activity to allow this child a chance to show what he can do.

Keep photographic evidence where this would be more informative than a written record.

- a picture of the model or collage with the child beside it
- a photo showing Sam balancing on top of the climbing frame
- a photograph of a group of children playing cooperatively in the shop, in their dressing up clothes.

Put the date and the stepping stone or early learning goal on the reverse and make a copy for each child involved. A digital camera will become an essential piece of your assessment kit.

Sharing assessment records

Make time each week to talk with your colleagues about the children. You may be the key worker, but any number of your colleagues will have worked with the children over the week. Raise any concerns you have about a particular child. Ask others if they have noticed anything. Plan for everyone to keep an eye on a particular child's behaviour or emotions the following week. Or ask everyone to watch, and if necessary correct, for example, Jordan's pencil grip, as this is one of his goals for next week. Discuss the level of challenge being offered to the children. Do you need to put out some more complex jigsaws? Would some finer paintbrushes help the older children to add more detail?

To sum up

- Assess what the children can already do, or already know.
- Assess what the children have learned.
- Assess how each child has learned or accessed the equipment.
- Assess children carrying out the same activity in different situations.

EVALUATION

Evaluation informs you about the suitability of the activity you set out. There are a number of questions which you should go through with your colleagues at the end of the week. These will help you to think about the activities you have offered the children and whether or not they did what you hoped they would do. Think about the activity, the learning intentions you had for that activity and what the children gained from it. Use your assessment records and your shared observations to answer these questions.

■ Did it work?

■ Why not?

■ What could we do to make it more effective?

■ Should we repeat this activity in an adapted way?

■ Should we abandon this idea?

■ Do we need to have this as an adult-led activity instead of free play?

■ If it worked, why did it work?

■ What made it particularly successful?

■ Could we use this approach with other activities?

Ask the questions about this activity. You wanted the children to practise cutting skills. You set out some paper plates, some scraps of paper and lengths of wool and expected them to make masks. The children didn't cut anything. They simply stuck bundles of wool on for hair, and tore the paper to make the features.

Look at each area of the nursery in turn as you go through the questions.

(You don't need to record it in this way. This is just to show you how the process works, and how your discussion might develop.)

AREA: house play **Activity:** dressing up clothes for a wedding		
Learning intention: to play cooperatively		
Did the children play cooperatively?	No	They were arguing about who should be the bride
Was there an adult in the house with the children at any time?	Yes	But only on Tuesday morning when we had a trainee here. We hadn't planned anyone to be in the house as we thought they could play on their own
Did the children play cooperatively when the the adult was present?	Yes	They needed someone to help them sort out the roles
What was our overall evaluation of this activity?	This was too advanced a theme for this intention; some children had never been to a wedding. If we do this again we need to plan for an adult to be in the house with the children to encourage cooperative play. We need to do more input with the children about role-play themes before expecting them to be able to enact things on their own. We need to make a more familiar theme the focus if we want the children to be cooperative.	

Handy Hints

- Plan and prepare your activities carefully.
- When you are delivering activities, you may take the role of facilitator, observer or instructor.
- Assessing activities allows you to discover what children already know and what they have learnt from those activities.
- Evaluating activities lets you know about the suitability of activities for the children involved.

CHAPTER 4

THE TEACHING ROOM

For most of the day you will be working as part of a team, and will be moving from indoor to outdoor areas, from one activity to another, working with children, facilitating or carrying out some practical tasks. You may be working with children in a play setting or you may be in charge of a number of tiny babies. This chapter will therefore reflect this and concentrate on the general need to provide a safe and caring space for children.

ATMOSPHERE

The atmosphere, or ethos, of your setting depends on the adults and on the boundaries for behaviour that you set.

POSITIVE ADULTS

It can be a stressful time for children when they leave the security of their homes and parents. It is therefore vitally important that from the moment they enter your setting they experience an atmosphere that is:

- supportive
- positive
- warm and welcoming.

This depends on the attitudes of the adults who work there.

Being supportive

Understand the other person first. Try to put yourself in their shoes.

> *If a mother arrives late to pick up her child, harassed because she has been held up in a traffic tail-back, offer sympathy first. Tell her you understand, tell her how you entertained her child whilst waiting, how you reassured the child that mummy would be here soon and so on. You want her to go away feeling that you provide a safe environment for her child to be in. She will recognise that how you treat her is a reflection of how you will be treating her child throughout the day.*

> *If Lucy is getting frustrated because she can't get the bricks to pile up high and she's crying when they fall down, don't add to the tension or fuel her frustration; sit calmly down with her, help her and then show her the fun of knocking the pile down. Maintain a calm and quiet voice, sit in a relaxed way, don't respond to her cross behaviour, just keep on building up the bricks, helping her to learn to put them more squarely one on top of another. Give her lots of praise.*

Being positive

Greet the child with a smile on your face – no matter how you feel. A true professional leaves her personal life at the door and puts on a professional face for the whole day. Look for the good in all children and the opportunities that different situations present.

At this stage, children don't always know the right way to behave. Part of your role is to help them to sort out appropriate from inappropriate responses. We will look at this in more detail in the section on behaviour, but remember that it is better to remain positive.

> *When Mario knocks over the pot of paint, respond in a calm way, 'Oh dear. Let's get a cloth and sort out this mess', not raising your voice and telling him off for making a mess.*

> *When Aaron throws a car across the room, he may not have realised that it could cause damage to another child. Tell him. Explain to him that some things are soft or light or bouncy − like the sponge balls. Show him one so that he knows what you are referring to − never simply assume that a child understands. Then explain that hard things like this car shouldn't be thrown. Use this opportunity to help him to learn and to increase his awareness and understanding of the world around him.*

Being warm and welcoming

Greet the children in a cheerful but professional way when they first arrive. Give them good eye-contact and make them feel that you are pleased to see them. Comment on the new coat, admire the little toy they have brought in. Check with the parent or carer that all is well. How's his cold today? Did he get a better night's sleep? Do you want us to give him his medicine today? Take an interest and show that you know and care about the child.

Throughout the day be accessible to the children. You are not there to chat with your colleagues. If you are speaking with them you will have to judge whether the child needs immediate attention – for example when Lee is being toilet trained and needs to go 'Now!' – or whether this is an opportunity for you to show the child that sometimes we have to wait our turn. If this is the case, be as brief as you can with the adult, holding the child's hand so that he knows you haven't forgotten him. Then turn to the child, thank him for waiting his turn, tell him that you appreciated his patience, and then respond to his request with total attention.

Whenever possible come down to a child's level. Squat down or sit on a small chair when talking to children, sit on the floor when they are working on the floor.

Be re-assuring. If there is a crisis keep calm so that the children know that you are in charge and that everything can be sorted and put back to normal. This could include removing a wasp from the room or carrying out a fire-drill.

If children are distressed, keep the atmosphere around them as calm as you can. Talk in a quiet soothing way until they can regain some composure. Hold their hand, or rest your hand on their shoulder just to let them know that you are there. When things are calming down a joke can be a good thing – the familiar to us, but new to children, jokes about 'Did you leave a big hole in the playground when you fell down?' usually work.

BOUNDARIES AND BEHAVIOUR

Children need boundaries. They need to know that there is a limit. If they know the boundary they can choose to play safely within it, or they can test it. Children don't understand about danger in the way that we do. They can't yet judge that things are sharp or hot as quickly as we can. Part of your role is to help them to acquire that ability. You do this by creating the risk, within a fixed boundary.

> *You plan an activity to make soup. This involves cutting up the vegetables. You provide the boundary – you choose vegetables that are not too hard, not too large and not too small. You provide knives that are sharp enough to do the job. You work with only a few children at a time so that you can keep an eye on everyone. You set the activity up away from areas where other children will be dashing around. The children then work with knives which is, broadly speaking, a risky activity.*

> *You have a climbing frame outside. You set boundaries in order to minimise the risk. You will have a smaller frame for under-twos, and a higher one for the older children. You will limit the number of children allowed on at any one time. An adult will always be near.*

Allowing some risk-taking

Children are programmed to take risks. If this weren't the case they would never develop many of their skills. When children try to push the boundaries you have set, you will have to think carefully about your response. Think about why they are pushing the boundary. Are they developmentally ready for the next step? Are they used to playing with older siblings and encouraged to take risks at home?

Then think about how you will respond. Let them try the bigger, more complex activity. Stay with the child, observe and assess. If he is ready and there is no reason for him not to play there, then let him go ahead.

If not ready, the child will probably be aware of this, maybe feeling scared when he gets to the top of the tall slide. Tell him he should stick to the original plan for now, but that he can try again next week. Make sure that you note this down and don't forget to do it.

If there is a reason for not crossing the boundary yet, perhaps the taller slide is in the garden area used by the older children, then be firm. Explain why he can't go there or do that thing. Don't give in, no matter how much begging, wailing or kicking goes on. Children have to learn that you are a secure and trustworthy person. When you say 'No', you must mean 'No'.

Your policy to promote positive behaviour

A behaviour policy should be there to explain how you will work to help the children learn the difference between appropriate and inappropriate behaviour. Use the policy to describe:

- the behaviours you want to see
- the behaviours you won't accept
- how you will respond to positive behaviour
- how you will respond to unacceptable behaviour.

Children often hear the words 'Don't do that', 'Don't touch that', 'Put that down' or 'Leave her alone'. They know what they shouldn't do. They also know that if they do that thing an adult will speak to them, will react to them, will make contact with them.

Catch them being good

Make it your practice to let the children know when they are doing the right thing. 'I like the way you are painting that so carefully.' 'That was kind, to let Jamie go first' 'Thank you for tidying up those bricks'. In this way the children will know when they are being good and that when they do these good things an adult will speak to them, will react to them and will make contact with them. Try to accompany this with ignoring the unacceptable behaviour if you can. Provided a child is not being hurt or the child is not going to do himself any harm, it is usually better to ignore silly behaviour, to find someone doing something that you can praise and do so in a clear way. This will have the effect of drawing attention away from the poor behaviour and away from the child who is trying to get your attention. He will soon make the connection that this other, better kind of behaviour gets your attention.

Following your policy on consequences to inappropriate behaviour

If you can't ignore the behaviour, then follow the agreed policy in your setting. Intervene so that no-one gets hurt, removing any offending article that is being used as a weapon. Tell the child that this (and describe the action precisely) should not be taking place. Be explicit so that the child hears exactly what he did wrong. Try to avoid general terms such as 'hurt' or 'not nice'. Be specific. 'Hitting Lara with a sharp brick has cut her hand'. 'Poking Ben with the pencil has left a bruise'. 'You made Pete cry when you took his toy away'.

Tell the child how he should have behaved and help him to do this now.

Another member of the staff team will have looked after the hurt child. Both children can now be encouraged to make friends again, saying sorry and shaking hands or giving each other a hug. Once dealt with, resume normal responses to both children. The incident happened, it was dealt with, it is over.

Time out

Repeated poor behaviour may need firmer responses. Time out (see Chapter One) is a safe and effective way of managing unwanted behaviour. Talk with the parents about what is happening and what you are doing to help their child learn a more appropriate way of behaving. Talk with them in confidence, away from other parents. Approach this with the parents in a positive way, helping then to see that this is simply a step along the way to behaving well, not as a dreadful event that demands punishment. Discuss ways in which they can reinforce the learning at home. They may be able to shed light on this situation and together you can find a way to address it.

Codes of conduct for all

It is important that the code of conduct you adopt should apply to all people who are in the setting. If the children can't run in the indoor space, then neither can you. If they are expected to speak in reasonable voices, without shouting, then so are all the adults. If the children have to change their shoes when they play outdoors, then so should you. Remember that the children are watching you and learning from you all the time. Behave at all times as you would want them to behave, showing respect for others and for their property.

To sum up

Create a positive atmosphere by having adults behave in ways that are:

- supportive
- positive
- warm and welcoming.

Set boundaries that:

- provide safe environments
- contain risk taking.

Have a behaviour policy that:

- encourages children to learn how to act, and how to respond in acceptable ways
- sets out measures to support those who are finding it difficult to behave in acceptable ways.

All staff and children should follow the agreed code of conduct for the setting.

THE SPACE

Consider how you use all the different parts of the setting:

- indoors and outdoors
- ancillary areas such as cloakrooms and bathrooms.

Indoor and outdoor areas

Some activities are obviously better suited to being set out indoors and others outdoors. Beyond this, think creatively. Your only constraints should be safety and supervision.

Use specific weather conditions as learning opportunities

- Ice in the water tray will stay frozen longer outside on cooler days: have warm water next to it and make sure that children regularly warm up their hands in this.
- Glue outside acts differently from glue inside.
- Paint dries faster outside on sunny days, but inside when the heating is switched on.
- Wrap up warmly and have a windy day story outside.
- Take the moulds and cutters outside if you have snow.

Use the space

Use the space outside to encourage greater involvement or to allow an activity to take up more space than you can allow it indoors:

- dressing up clothes
- house play
- painting or collage on huge sheets of paper or fabric
- big building or construction sets
- huge boxes from your supermarket or cylindrical inner rolls from a carpet shop.

Placing some of these traditionally indoor activities outdoors will also free up the indoor space.

Whatever activities you carry out outside, remember that outside play is not the equivalent of playtime in a school, but should be seen as another area of learning in your setting. Whatever is outside should be as well planned as the activities indoors, and the children should be observed, supported, taught and assessed on their learning wherever they are playing.

Ancillary areas such as bathrooms and cloakrooms

Your first priorities in these areas should be the health and safety of all who use them, and general hygiene. The areas should be kept clean and tidy at all times.

- Keep supplies available and use them correctly and safely.
- List any children who have allergies or need particular soaps or creams, and pin this to the wall above the changing mats so that you are reminded each time you are in there.
- Older children should be supervised and allowed time to learn about the rules of toilet flushing and hand washing.
- Mop up any spills immediately.
- Keep cloakrooms free of clutter. If hooks are blocked with bulky coats, provide bins or bags for spare shoes or clothes. Have pegs with names on to keep wellingtons in pairs.

This is an important place where children will learn and practise some of their new skills and achievements. Treat it as such, helping the children to acquire steps towards independence and praising them for their achievements.

Over the day you may be expected to work in any of these areas in your setting. Look for the opportunities each area presents to facilitate learning, to connect with the children and to take care of the space and the equipment within it.

DISPLAYS

Displays can have different purposes. They can be:

- For information: information for parents on what you are doing this week, alerting parents to the presence of head-lice, notes to staff about allergy or medicine.

- To record learning: here are the paintings we did this morning, these photos show us when we went to the farm.

- To encourage the children to interact: which animal is under this silhouette? Lift the flap and look. Have you found something blue for our table this week?

- Ever-changing and on-going: this is where we put the stories which the children write.

- For educational purposes: an alphabet or number chart that children can use to help them.

Look around your setting and see if you can recognise the purposes of the displays you have set up. Try to maintain a balance of the types of display so that you know that you are covering all the potential uses.

Some simple rules for display

- Colour-coordinate the backing paper, the mounts and the labels with each other and with the children's work so that it is shown off to maximum impact.

- Repair or change any torn or damaged items, or backing paper.

- Replace the whole display on a regular basis. Don't let it become simply wallpaper.

- Share the task of setting up displays, as they are time consuming to do, but also because people have their own style – much as we have a handwriting style – and it is better to encourage variety.

- Check that displays are visible to the children. Get down on your knees and check this out. This is especially relevant to table-top displays.
- Never use anything which could harm a child in any way, or that would upset the owner if it were to get damaged or broken.
- Make sure that labels are well written and correctly spelt. Use a computer if you are unsure. Don't forget to use capitals only for names and the start of sentences.

RESOURCES

There are three things to be aware of at all times with resources. They should be:

- **Accessible.** Children should be able to reach and recognise those things you want them to use. A piece of the construction kit or an old jigsaw piece sellotaped to the edge of the box will allow the children to recognise the contents and so choose easily. Stick a piece of the equipment to the shelf where it is kept so that the children can replace it after use. If there are things that children shouldn't be touching, make sure they are in a locked cupboard or on high shelves.
- **Appropriate.** Think about the safety of your resources, and also about hidden messages of gender, ability or race discrimination. Look at your learning goal and check that this activity or toy will allow the children to learn this.
- **Well maintained.** Check equipment as you put it away. Have a place for damaged goods and repair things as soon as you have time. Keep equipment clean and in order. Everyone should take some responsibility for this. If you

need specific skills such as woodwork or sewing to repair
something, ask your children's parents. Large climbing
equipment should be meticulously checked each day. Sand
should be replaced regularly and sieved each day. Water
should be replaced every day.

To sum up

Displays should:

- have a clear purpose
- be changed regularly
- be well presented.

Resources should be:
- accessible
- appropriate
- well-maintained.

Handy Hints

- You cannot underestimate the importance of welcoming atmosphere and positive adults.
- Set boundaries and promote positive behaviour.
- Staff and children need to be aware of and abide by codes of conduct.
- Manage your space, including indoor and outdoor areas and cloakrooms.
- Make the best of displays and resources.

CHAPTER 5

WORKING WITH COLLEAGUES AND PARENTS OR CARERS

Everyday, as well as working with the children, you are communicating with adults, and those adults comprise three main groups: your colleagues, the parents or carers of the children in your care and other professionals. To do this well you need to exercise your interpersonal skills.

INTERPERSONAL SKILLS

Simply put, these are the skills that allow you to communicate effectively with other people. They are the skills of:

- establishing trust with the other person
- exploring and responding to their needs
- postponing your judgment or response until you have heard the full story
- not assuming you know what the other person is trying to say or how they are feeling.

Do you have these skills?

Think about people whom you trust. What is it about them, their words, actions or responses, that lets you feel this trust? Reflect on what they do or say. Do you behave like this to other people?

Think about someone that you don't trust. Why not? What do they say or how do they behave that stops you trusting them? Do you ever behave like this?

Do your friends or colleagues treat you as someone who is trustworthy?

- Are you able to support people, to help them to see the best way forward for them?
- Do you listen to people without interrupting, or giving them your opinion before you've heard the full story?
- Are you able to listen without turning the focus to yourself and your own experience?
- Do you let the other person have plenty of time to present the whole picture to you?
- Are you able to use prompting questions, to make sure that you do have the whole picture, without diverting the flow of the other person's concerns?
- Do you listen without assuming that you know all the answers?

If you can do all of these things then you are probably a good 'people person' and have strong interpersonal skills.

WORKING WITH COLLEAGUES

Sharing good practice in your setting

If you want to build up your strengths you can go on courses, but a cheaper option is to use the varying skills of those you work with. Everyone has something that they do well, and it is a good work habit to share these skills with your team. The person with the skill has to analyse what they are doing well, and plan how to explain or demonstrate this to the rest of the team. It makes that person feel professionally valued. The rest of the team sees some sound professional practice in action. They can see its benefits, they can ask questions, or work alongside their colleague to practise it for themselves. Overall, standards of practice will improve in your setting.

How do we do this?

Here are some case studies to show how sharing good practice could work for you.

Case study 1

Andy is working in a setting which takes in children from a socially disadvantaged area. Some parents have problems with drink and drugs and can be quite abusive to staff. He has noticed that one of his colleagues, Sally, is very good at calming situations down, whereas some others have great problems dealing with these parents. He asks Sally what her secret is. She explains to him, he tries her approach next time he is in this situation, and it works. Impressed, he talks to Sally and the nursery manager and asks if Sally could share her approach with all of the staff in one of their weekly meetings. This happens and soon the incidents that do occur are handled so much better by everyone and there is generally a better atmosphere at the start and close of the day. This has now become part of the induction programme and Sally talks to all new staff or trainees about what has become the accepted approach.

Case study 2

Angie took on the responsibility for the three-year-olds at an established nursery. The previous nursery nurse had run it in an autocratic way – she was in charge, she knew what was best and everyone did as she directed. When Angie asked about the weekly plans, nobody knew how to prepare them. For years they had been given the plan and had worked to it. Angie called a meeting of all staff who worked in the room. She showed them the format that she was accustomed to using, along with copies of the existing format and others she had collected from other settings. She encouraged the staff to talk about why they needed a plan, what information they felt should be on it and the most effective way of presenting it. Angie took notice of all the ideas and together the team came up with a format that suited them all. At the end of the session the staff had started to work together, each feeling that their contribution was useful and of value. They had started to become a team. There was a long way to go, but Angie had started off the process by using her interpersonal skills and by valuing everyone.

It would have been very easy for Angie to use the format she had used before, to simply hand it over to this team of people who were used to being compliant. By involving everyone and making it a team process, Angie was encouraging each person to practise new skills, to share their knowledge and to work together.

Case study 3

Chris went on a course called Modelling Maths to find out new ways of using recycled materials to introduce mathematical concepts. She was full of enthusiasm for it when she returned to the nursery the next day, and she explained it to her colleagues during their weekly meeting. It was decided that over the following week she would use some of the ideas each day, and set the maths area out accordingly. Each member of the team was allocated some time (one person each day) to watch Chris with the children. At the following week's team meeting they all talked about the benefits they had noticed and at how the children had been enthused by the ideas. They agreed to plan more ideas around this and slot the ideas into the future weekly plans.

Working with other professionals

Over time you will work with many other professionals, and this means those who are other than nursery nurses. You may have to work with healthcare professionals. Speech and language therapists, physiotherapists and occupational therapists may be working with some of your special needs children. The doctor, school nurse or a member of the Child and Adolescent Mental Health services team may need to talk with you about one of the children in your care. Or you may be working alongside social care professionals. It is important that you respect their shared concerns for the children and at the same time recognise your individual professional strengths. To do this you must first of all know your own role, and your areas of expertise, and then value others and their skills.

Know your own role

Your job description should sum up your role and your responsibilities within your setting. Be aware of these. If you go beyond this agreed role and make an error of judgment, there could be serious professional consequences. If you feel ready to take on more responsibility, then do this in the correct way, through appraisal, professional development opportunities or by applying for another position, rather than by treading on the toes of others. Recognise the many skills you do have and be prepared to share those skills with colleagues, trainees or other professionals when you are discussing the needs of a child.

Value others and their skills

Make it your business to know who does what, so that you can refer to the correct professional for help and advice in circumstances that are beyond your own area of expertise. This might be a colleague who is more experienced than you, or who has senior responsibility, or it may be a member of another profession. You may be talking with parents when they raise issues that you know are beyond your remit. Point this out to them and suggest the name or profession of the person who could give more appropriate help or advice.

Confidentiality or information sharing

When dealing with other professionals be aware of the need for confidentiality. There may be family situations that you have been told about by the parent in confidence. Don't break this. If the other professional needs to know, go back to the parent and explain why they ought to share this information and then leave it to them. You could offer to be with them when they explain, if this would help them.

INVOLVING PARENTS OR CARERS

In this section we will be thinking about involving parents or carers in two broad ways:

- the everyday, practical involvement that occurs when they leave or collect children or attend parent meetings
- the planned involvement of parents in their children's learning.

Regular, ongoing involvement

More than at any other time in the child's education you will have opportunities to build a relationship with a child's parents and carers. The benefits of making this a positive relationship are well documented, and can be summed up as:

- Parents or carers are the most significant adults in a child's life.
- Parents or carers are the child's first educators.
- Children benefit when there is a coordinated approach to their care.

Information sharing

When parents or carers come to look round your nursery before they make their final choice, this first meeting with the parent or carer can set the tone for your future relationship. Make sure that you allow time so that you are not rushing through the meeting, and privacy so that you are not interrupted. Prepare for the meeting, getting together all of the paperwork which you might need and anything you want the parents to take away with them.

Think about what the parents or carers might want to know as well as what they need to know. Sit with them in your office or another quiet space and give them a broad picture of how the nursery is run and how you operate. Explain what it is that sets your nursery apart from others. Then show them round, pointing out examples of what you have talked about. Return to your office, offer the parents or carers some coffee, discuss routines, expectations, fees and all the practical considerations, and answer their questions.

When the child is due to start with you

This meeting should revolve around the child and his needs. Find out from the parents or carers about:

- health matters, allergies, medical conditions
- food preferences – think about cultural needs and norms, allergies
- home routines for discipline, and how these can be matched with your own behaviour policy. Talk this through and reach a mutual agreement
- day-time sleep routines including time, position and favourite toy
- toilet routines.

Tell the parents or carers about:

- daily routines
- any curriculum information
- clothes, meals and other practical information
- behaviour expectations and responses.

This discussion will set the tone, by showing parents or carers that you respect what they have done, and are still doing, for their child. Explain that your intention is to build on this and to add other skills linked to social learning. These are skills which the child will need when he is part of a larger group, with a smaller adult to child ratio than exists in the home.

Daily, informal meetings with parents or carers take place every day. Allow time for these. Ask about the child in the morning, and through a general conversation find out if he has been unwell or up late. Parents or carers who know that you take an interest will let you know if you can expect their child to be especially excited or fractious today. Make sure that you respond to this at the end of the day, letting the parent or carer know how the child was, and of any interventions you had to make. Have a list of adults who will be collecting children that day, if it is to be someone different from the norm, as this helps to keep children safe. Parents will value this. If parents are late collecting their child, be supportive. It may not have been their fault and they may be anxious when they turn up. Let them see you as a caring person.

Parents' or carers' meetings have a more formal tone to them, but that doesn't have to mean that you are uncaring. Make notes of what you want to tell them. Note down ideas for things they may want to do at home to reinforce behaviour or learning, but be sensitive to the ability and time commitments of parents and carers. Allow time for them to ask you questions. If you don't have time to respond fully, or you want to find something out (perhaps a contact number for a professional who could offer more support), make a note and set up another meeting time with the parents or carers. Do it there and then. You will find a useful section on interacting with parents and carers in *Good Practice in the Early Years* (Kay, 2004).

Planned involvement of parents or carers

Planned involvement can be as simple as inviting a parent or carer in to share their skills: digging over the garden ready to plant some potatoes with the children, baking cakes for a special occasion or making huge sculptures in the outdoor area. It can be sending books home to share with the family. It can be inviting parents to sit on fund-raising committees or to lead or support a project to redesign the outdoor areas.

Brainstorm with your colleagues all the opportunities that arise in your setting where parents or carers could help out. Ignore the help they will give their own child, concentrate on help for the whole setting. Collate the list and organise it into:

- Help from home: some parents may be willing to take some dressing-up clothes home to wash and iron.
- Help on site: some parents may be able to come in and fit the new climbing frame together or repair the existing one, or to set up a new programme on the computer.
- Help with resources: cover the books, label the drawers.
- Help with activities during the sessions: making pizza, sewing.
- Help with children: reading to small groups, additional lunch time help for a child with special needs.
- Help with events: sitting on a committee, selling raffle tickets, setting up and running stalls.
- Help with visits: coming with you on visits in the locality or further afield.

There should be something here for everyone, whatever their home and work commitments. Include this in your parent information pack and ask parents or carers to indicate if, how and when they could help. Let them know that this list is not

exhaustive and you welcome their offers of help beyond these ideas.

There are some campaigns to involve parents and carers in their children's learning. These are usually aimed at those living in disadvantaged areas or areas of poor socioeconomic standing, but you could take some of their well-researched and successful ideas, and adapt them for your own setting.

Raising Early Achievement in Literacy

This project started at the University of Sheffield in collaboration with Sheffield Local Education Authority. It aimed to help children's literacy by 'enhancing the roles of parents in providing literacy opportunities, recognising their children's literary achievements, interacting with their children around literacy and being a model of a literacy user themselves.' A further focus was on adults' own literacy.

Details of how this was carried out and many ideas on how you could engage parents in their children's literary development are in *Early Literacy Work with Families. Policy, Practice and Research* (Nutbrown *et al*, 2005).

Other projects arose from this work, and versions of it, large and small, are being used around the world.

Peers Early Education Partnership

The Peers Early Education Partnership (PEEP) was started in Oxford but has extended into other areas (www.peep.org.uk). At first it was a literacy programme, but now includes aspects of self-esteem and numeracy. Parents and carers are supported in their homes and there are weekly sessions delivered in pre-school settings and foundation stage classes in schools. Parents and carers are able to access free resources to help them with this programme. The aim is that children will be able to take full advantage of the learning offered when they enter into full-time school.

Contact PEEP to arrange an information day in your area. You need a group of between 12 and 30 people and there is a small charge per person. Representatives will talk to you about the programme, introduce the resources and help you to plan how you can go forward.

Handling criticism or complaint

There will be times when things go wrong and you may receive complaints or criticism from a parent or even a group of parents or a colleague. When people are upset they may be aggressive or abusive. The most effective response to this is to remain calm and in control, no matter what you are feeling underneath. Let the person have their say to get it all off their chest and then invite them in to sit down, maybe have a cup of tea and go through it all again with less emotion; explain that you want to understand the facts and get things in order.

Working by the rules

Within your setting you will have a set of rules that everyone has to abide by. They are there for the safety and support of all who work, learn and play there. At home there will be a different set of rules. Children have to learn that this is the way of the world and that different places need different rules and that they are all important. Parents and carers sometimes come into conflict with nurseries when they fail to appreciate this. You have to listen to their complaint and then explain clearly and simply, but not in any condescending way, that you and the children have to go along with the agreed rules here. If you have set these out clearly in your brochure, have explained them to parents when they came to register their child with you, and if you have child-friendly codes of conduct posted around the setting, this will make your task much easier.

Negotiating skills

- listen to both sides
- try to see both sides' points of view
- remain calm in manner and voice
- be polite
- identify a compromise that allows each person to have dignity.

Complaints procedure

You need to have a complaints procedure. This should be written down and be available to all staff and all parents and carers. Like an insurance policy, it's good to have one and we all hope never to have to use it. Make sure that you know what it is in your setting.

If a parent or carer complains, record their complaint while they are present, and both of you sign it. Agree your next action. This might be to schedule a meeting to talk it out, or to inform your line manager.

Deal with all complaints fairly and quickly. Give yourself time to hear all the facts before you commit yourself to an action or response which you might later regret.

Above all else, try to avoid reaching the stage where a formal complaint is made. Keep parents or carers informed at the earliest opportunity about any problem with their child or any potential change to routines or fees. Involving them early on can prevent an escalation of emotional responses.

To sum up

- Develop good interpersonal skills.
- Value your colleagues.
- Share good practice.
- Value other professionals and their specific skills and knowledge.
- Know your own role and when to ask for help and advice.
- Value parents and carers.
- Involve parents and carers from the very beginning.
- Consider ways to include parents and carers in the setting and in their own children's learning.
- Deal with conflict or complaint in a fair, calm and just way.

Handy Hints

- Identify and develop your interpersonal skills to make sure you are communicating properly with everyone.
- Working with colleagues is vital to share good practice and support each other.
- Working with other professionals is important as you all have shared concerns for the children.
- Involve parents and carers in their children's learning – look at the Raising Early Achievement in Literacy programme and Peers Early Education Partnership for further ideas.
- You will inevitably be faced with criticism or complaint at some point – try to stay calm and make sure you have all the facts before you respond. You should have a complaints procedure to follow in this instance – make sure you know what it is.

CHAPTER 6

LOOKING AFTER YOURSELF

SAFEGUARDING YOUR PHYSICAL HEALTH

Your job is physically demanding and you will have to take steps
to keep fit if you are to continue to be able to do it well.

Looking after yourself

Make sure that your lifestyle is a healthy one.

- Eat and drink sensibly. A balanced diet, with plenty of fresh
  fruit and vegetables, and a limit to snacks and junk foods
  will build up your immune system and allow your body to
  fight off the many germs - coughs, colds and tummy bugs
  - that the children will bring into the setting.
- Keep active. Walking is good exercise and most people
  should be able to find time to do this. If you have sporting
  interests keep these up for as long as you can. Aerobics, line
  dancing, or swimming, whatever you choose, make sure
  that you enjoy it. As an added bonus you may be able to
  socialise at the same time.
- Keep fit. Try to give up smoking, limit your alcohol intake
  and be sensible about your weight.
- To balance this you need plenty of rest. A good night's
  sleep makes the whole world seem brighter.

Remember, '... exercise improves general well-being and health'.
(Blakemore and Frith, 2005).

Stay safe at work

Know the health and safety measures you should follow at work.

Know the whereabouts of the first aid box. Those who administer first aid should have a recognised certificate. Is yours up-to-date? Who is in charge of keeping the first aid box topped up? Do any of the children or staff have allergies that you should know about? Record all interventions even if they seem minor at the time.

Fire safety and other emergency procedures should be practised by everyone on a regular basis. Make sure that you know what these procedures are, and who is responsible for what. Think of these scenarios.

- You have always taught the children to leave the room by a certain exit, but the fire is near that exit.
- Maxine always collects the register when you have a fire drill. She is away from work when there is a fire.
- You smell gas.

Always wear gloves for messy jobs, especially when dealing with bodily fluids. Wash your hands thoroughly afterwards with an anti-bacterial liquid soap and then dry your hands well. Germs like warm and damp conditions.

Attend courses on lifting techniques to avoid straining your back. If you have children with physical difficulties, take advice from the physiotherapists involved with the child. They will be able to show you how to lift the child onto a changing mat, or in and out of a wheelchair, in ways that will be safe and comfortable for the child as well as good for the long-term health of your back.

Wear sensible clothing and shoes. You need to look smart as you are a professional person. But you do need to be able to climb up the frame to rescue George, who is clinging on and daren't come down, or crawl under a table to disentangle Susie and her bridal veil from the buckle on Sami's new shoes, and tiptoe through a whole group of children working on the floor to reach Adam, without piercing anyone's hand with the heels of your shoes.

Check that the room is safe for the children to play and learn in. Anything you do to protect them is also going to protect you. Carry out a risk assessment of the workplace, both indoors and out. Look for sharp edges, splinters, holes and tears. Put these right as soon as you can, or tape the area off until it can be fixed. Put corner protectors on where necessary, or buffers on doors to prevent trapped fingers. If you can show that you have the interests of the children at the heart in all that you do, and that you are aware of the potential risks and have made every effort to minimise those risks and have recorded this fact, then no-one should be able to accuse you of neglect or of failing in your duty of care to the children.

Know about child protection procedures, and familiarise yourself with the rules on restraining children. These rules should always be obeyed to the letter. Any breach can leave you open to accusations.

MAINTAINING YOUR EMOTIONAL HEALTH

The emotions are an intrinsic and important part of each of us, and along with our physical condition make us what we are.

Support systems

Never be afraid to ask for help. Don't struggle on by yourself, getting deeper and deeper into despair or helplessness. No problem or situation is as bad as you see it. A more experienced colleague will help you to get things sorted out and will show you the bigger picture. You can be helped to work through a problem and shown how to find appropriate help and advice.

You may be a lone nursery nurse working in a school. It is always good to have others with whom you can share your specific concerns. Are there any support groups in your area for nursery nurses working in school? Similar groups exist in the educational establishments for heads and special educational needs coordinators. If there isn't one for nursery nurses, send a flyer round to all the local schools and find out if there is any interest, and then set one up. Meet up once a month after school, and have a coffee and a chat. If you can't find other nursery nurses in your local schools, ask the early years teacher you work with if she attends a support group and if you can go along to their meetings.

Mentor systems

When you first start at a nursery or school you are entitled to an induction period. You may also be allocated a member of the existing staff as your mentor. Take full advantage of this. Your mentor is there to answer your questions. If you don't understand, ask. If you can't find something, ask. Raise issues that are worrying you and talk through your concerns.

When you meet your line manager to talk about your progress, perhaps as part of your appraisal, use this time to air any concerns. 'I'm good at this, but I would like to learn more about that'. 'I am struggling with this, is there any chance of any additional support or training?'

Keeping everything in perspective

See difficulties as opportunities to learn and grow. Take account of where you are in your development as a nursery nurse, and give yourself permission to be not quite perfect ...yet.

Know what you need to work on and what skills and knowledge you have yet to learn. Set about this learning with confidence. Use the appraisal system as a chance to focus on yourself and your professional needs. Look out for courses or additional training that you can undertake. Set aside the time to do this. Don't simply add it to an already packed schedule. Plan your learning, plan the time to read, to study, complete assignments or to do any follow up thinking.

Don't punish yourself if something is beyond you: either see the opportunity to develop your skills and knowledge, or acknowledge that it's not for you, with no shame or guilt or sense of failure, but with a positive sense of setting clear boundaries for yourself.

Marie was an experienced nursery nurse. She had worked in the setting for almost ten years, knew the routines well and was popular with the children and their parents. Her colleagues respected her skills, and liked her as a person. The manager was taken sick and was to be away for some time, and Marie was asked to take on her role until she was well enough to return. Everything went well; Marie handled all the situations that arose, welcomed new children and their parents, dealt with all the day-to-day crises that arise in every setting, and handed the reins back to the manager when she came back to work. No-one knew that Marie had hardly slept for those eight weeks. She had hated the responsibility even though it was well within her capabilities. She decided that management wasn't for her.

Value yourself. Know what you are good at and give yourself credit for these skills and the knowledge that you have about children, their development and their needs. You can feel good by doing this, and by recognising your contribution to the children's education and wellbeing. You can do lots of what you're good at, but make room for developing other skills and strengths.

You love working in the baby room, and you have been told how well you do this. Working with the three-year-olds still worries you, although you would like to try working with this group to extend your professional skills. Ask if you can spend some time with these older children, while maintaining your position in the baby room. Attend some courses and talk to your colleagues who are experienced with this age group. By extending your range of skills in this way you will be ready to make the move when it is available.

At the end of the day give yourself a metaphorical pat on the back by reviewing the good things you have done for the children today.

STRESS BUSTING TIPS AND ADVICE

First let's define stress. Stress is our response to demands placed on us in our daily lives. Some stress is normal, even good. It causes us to feel afraid or anxious in some situations and prepares us to fight or to run away from the potential danger. But if any situation is causing us an abnormally high level of unease, or bodily tension and it becomes more than we can cope with, we can suffer from stress.

These things which cause stress are known as stressors. They can be external or internal. The external stressors can include aspects of our physical surroundings such as noise. They can also be poor working conditions, negative interactions with those around us at home or at work, and major life changes.

Internal stressors can be poor nutrition, lack of consistency or rhythm to your working day, lack of fulfilment and unresolved conflicts. Stress at work can be caused by time pressure, workload, feeling undervalued by others or by a lack of team spirit.

How will you know if you are suffering from stress? You could have physical illnesses, especially digestive or respiratory problems or skin disorders. You could have headaches, panic attacks or difficulties in sleeping. You may feel agitated, panicky or irritable, or you may tire easily. You may well find yourself snacking, overeating, drinking or smoking more than is usual for you. You may also find yourself overworking, unable to know when to stop.

There may be things you can change about your work place or the relationships among your colleagues. This would benefit you, it would also help others and make the setting a better place to work in; ideas in Chapter 5 could help with this. You can definitely do things for yourself that will help you to combat stressful situations.

Look after yourself

- Allow time to eat.
- Eat a diet high in fruit and vegetables.
- Avoid sugary or starchy food.
- Take some exercise each day.
- Try relaxation programmes such as yoga or meditation.

Modify your lifestyle

- Develop friendships, especially outside work.
- Take up some hobbies and interests.
- Get a life – socialise.
- Deal with family issues at home as soon as possible.

Be pro-active at work

- Deal with problems immediately.
- Prioritise jobs – do the hardest one first.
- Recognise your own limitations. Learn to say 'No' and don't feel guilty about it.
- Get support and advice from a mentor or line manager, or from a more experienced colleague.
- Don't be afraid to ask for help, advice or support.
- Look for ways to keep your work interesting.

Develop a positive attitude

- Be objective. Don't let emotions overwhelm you. Step back from a situation and think it through.
- Be in control. Set yourself clear goals for work or study, with time boundaries, and stick to them.
- Be open. Don't bottle up your feelings, talk to someone.
- Use distraction or thought-blocking techniques. When worrying thoughts are pressuring you, switch to a more positive, successful thought or achievement.
- Don't dramatise things. 'Everything's going wrong' No, it isn't. This particular thing may be going wrong but this and this and this are all fine.

And finally learn to laugh at yourself. Give yourself permission to be stupid.

Laugh, laugh and then laugh some more. In *The Brain's Behind It*, Alistair Smith (2002) describes the findings of research into laughter as a process that can reduce stress, improve sleep, aid learning, improve our general performance and enable us to deal better with cognitive challenges.

In conclusion

And so we see the importance of the life-work balance. You have chosen an exciting, difficult and challenging career. Give yourself credit for being prepared to take on the role of caring for and educating little children, but at the same time have a good life outside work, recharge your batteries, understand that there is more to life than work and value other aspects of your life.

And be proud of yourself.

Handy Hints

- Look after your physical health, including your diet, activity levels and lifestyle.
- Look after your emotional health. Ensure you have good support systems, keep everything in perspective and be positive.
- Stay safe at work.
- Aim for a good work–life balance.

BIBLIOGRAPHY

REFERENCES

Abbott L, Langston A, eds (2005) *Birth to Three Matters. Supporting the Framework of Effective Practice.* Open University Press, Maidenhead

Blakemore S-J, Frith U (2005) *The Learning Brain.* Blackwell Publishing, Oxford

Department for Education and Skills (2002) *Birth to Three Matters: A framework to support children in their earliest years.* Ref: BIRTH. DfES Publications Centre, Annesley, Nottingham

Department for Education and Skills (2003) *Every Child Matters.* Green Paper. DfES Publications Centre, Annesley, Nottingham

Kay J (2004) *Good Practice in the Early Years.* 2nd edn. Continuum, London

Nutbrown C, Hannon P, Morgan A (2005) *Early Literacy Work with Families. Policy, Practice and Research.* Sage Publications Limited, London

Qualifications and Curriculum Authority (2000) *Curriculum guidance for the Foundation Stage.* Ref: QCA/00/587. QCA Publications, Sudbury, Suffolk

Smith A (2002) *The Brain's Behind It.* Network Educational Press Limited, Stafford

FURTHER READING

Corrie C (2003) *Becoming Emotionally Intelligent.* Network Educational Press Limited, Stafford

Cousins L, Jennings J (2003) *The Positive Behaviour Handbook.* pfp Publishing, London

Cowley S (2005) *You can...Create a Calm Classroom.* Scholastic, Leamington Spa

Drake J (2001) *Planning Children's Play and Learning in the Foundation Stage.* David Fulton Publishers, London

Harker J (2003) 100 *Language games for ages 3–5.* Scholastic, Leamington Spa

Harrison P (2003) *An eye for display.* Belair, Dunstable

Honey P (2002) *Improve your people skills.* Chartered Institute of Personnel and Development, London

Hudson H (1992) *The Perfect Appraisal.* Random House Business Books, London

QCA (2001) *Planning for learning in the Foundation Stage.* Ref: QCA/01/799. QCA Publications, Sudbury, Suffolk

QCA (2003) *Foundation Stage Profile.* Ref: QCA/03/1006. QCA Publications, Sudbury, Suffolk

Riley J, ed. (2003) *Learning in the Early years. A guide for teachers of children 3-7.* Paul Chapman Publishing, London

Sharp A (2002) *100 Learning games for ages 0–3.* Scholastic, Leamington Spa

Sharp A (2004) *100 Our senses games for ages 0–3.* Scholastic, Leamington Spa

Whiteford R, Fitzsimmons J (1999) *Hands on display.* Belair, Dunstable

USEFUL WEBSITES

All accessed February 2006.

www.early-education.org.uk Publications to order, mainly centred on children's development in all its different forms, for example, emotional or creative development.

www.everychildmatters.gov.uk *Every Child Matters* – there are many documents aimed at different aspects of children's care and education. You can see them all on this site and download whatever you require.

www.folens.com Visit this site for details of a series entitled 'Belair Early Years' with books devoted to aspects of the curriculum, such as Art and ICT, and other general topics. They also have many well illustrated books on display.

www.foundationstage.net This site has areas dedicated to information about the foundation stage, the areas of learning and inspection information.

www.ltl.org.uk Learning Through Landscapes is an organisation which will provide help and advice on ways to maximise the use of the outdoor spaces in your setting.

www.mentalhealth.org.uk From this site you can download an A4 poster entitled: ways to look after your mental health. Pin this up on your staff notice board to remind all members of your team of the importance of looking after themselves.

www.ndna.org.uk the website for the National Day Nurseries Association. The new *National Occupational Standards* can be downloaded from this site.

www.peep.org.uk Visit this site for information, background and details of training on the Peers Early Education Partnership programme.

www.pre-school.org.uk There are several books related to inclusion which are published for Pre-school Alliance, available to buy online.

www.qca.org.uk You can download various QCA publications from this website.

www.standards.dfes.gov.uk You can download various DfES publications from this website.

www.surestart.gov.uk Download or read on-line regular newsletters with a range of information about news items to keep you up-to-date.

www.teachernet.gov.uk Follow the links: Teaching and Learning, Foundation Stage, Foundation Stage Resources to *Foundation Stage Forum*. Here you will find an online community with articles, policies, documents, e.g. NVQ3 guidance and a chance to discuss issues with your colleagues around the country. Some items are available generally, some are only for members at a cost of £20 per year.

www.underfives.co.uk This site provides planning and activities galore, themes, crafts, details of events and festivals month by month, handwriting sheets and much more. There are also links to other relevant professional, business and educational sites.